THE DAY SECRETARIAT WON THE TRIPLE CROWN

And the impact on a young disabled girl

A story of pain, heartbreak and triumph

Carolyn R Scheidies

C$_R$ Publications

Carolyn R. Scheidies

415 E 15th
Kearney, NE 68847-6959
(308) 234-3849
crscheidies@hotmail.com
Subject Line: Hope/Secretariat

I DEAL IN HOPE
History, Mystery, Romance...and Hope
http://IDealinHope.com/

© 2007, 2015 By Carolyn R. Scheidies
Cover Design: Carolyn R Scheidies
All Rights Reserved
2nd Printing

ISBN 978-0-6151-5964-5
http://www.lulu.com/content/897985

Scheidies BIO

A graduate from the University of Nebraska at Kearney (UNK) with a degree in journalism, Carolyn R. Scheidies' published credits include over two-dozen books, several of which have garnered awards. She's written for a variety of publications, has a regular newspaper column, worked as an editor, speaker/teacher and book reviewer and, wrote for Harlequin Heartsong Presents.

Scheidies speaks to different groups, leads workshops, lectured at UNK for several years and has taught adult enrichment writing classes at Central Community College. She has been interviewed on NTV, KHAS and AFR radio as well as in numerous print and online publications and had a monthly book review segment on NTV when she was a regular book reviewer. http://IDealinHope.com.

TABLE OF CONTENTS

CHAPTER ONE-The Beginning

The news of Secretariat's death made me realize how far removed I had become from my youthful obsession with horses, especially with Secretariat, a horse I had never even seen. It had been a long time since I'd even thought of him or how important he had been to me that spring.

The tentative rays of the afternoon sun lengthened the shadows in my small, square bedroom. I sat on my bed on the thick, warm, pink comforter-spread Dad brought home from Canada where he pastored a church. The windows on two sides of the room were covered with the white dotted pink curtains my older sister Karin lovingly made for me.

In one corner was the large desk Dad made for me several years earlier that was high enough for me to sit at in my wheelchair. In fact, I was surrounded with things that gave me security and attested to the care and concern of my family. The room itself was my secure little hide-away in a world that spun crazily. Even after all these months, I still felt bemused and not a little confused over the major events that had recently transpired.

Karin and her husband Jim had been transferred from McPherson, Kansas way out east to Maryland. There was the possibility of surgery for me. And then came the sudden death of my mother. My college graduation was not the same without Mom cheering me on as she had so diligently over the years.

The decision for or against surgery weighed heavily on my mind. Surgery might change my entire future, and I was in no state to make such a momentous decision.

It was June 1973. I turned 23 in January and graduated from college in May. Looking ahead, I was frightened, perhaps more frightened than I had ever been. And I had been frightened many times in the past ten years. Frightened and alone I perched on the edge of life, but for me that edge appeared to be more a dangerous precipice.

Crippled (why try to disguise the truth with the latest politically correct term) and able to move my wheelchair about only with my feet, I faced major surgery on legs that had not functioned properly for ten years. They were permanently bent and my fingers were gnarled from the ravages of Juvenile Rheumatoid Arthritis, which one way or another affected all parts of my slim body. Surgery might get me walking again--might. Knee replacements were fairly new and using them on someone my age was not recommended. My sympathetic doctor and friend, Dr. Ken Ellis, gave me no guarantees.

Was it worth it? It was my life--and my decision. Did I want to walk again? Of course! But what if I went through all the surgery and was no better? I thought. I prayed and was still not settled in mind or heart. My odds for success were a whole lot less than Secretariat's odds of winning the Kentucky Derby. I smiled as I turned my thoughts to the large horse. Horses. Nothing else could turn my mind as quickly from my present problems than horses.

From my earliest years I loved horses. More than once I heard Dad crack, "The day she was born, she began crawling toward horses."

"Completely horse crazy," was my sister's pronouncement, and she was right.

I loved horses. When we lived in Clitherall, Minnesota, some members of Dad's church had a farm that I loved to visit. To my delight, I even got to stay at the farm when Mom went to the hospital to have my younger brother Paul in 1954. I was four at the time.

They also had a very gentle horse. A few times, they lifted me up on its broad back, and, though I was hardly more than a toddler, I loved it.

I recall going to the Minneapolis State Fair with my Grandmother and Aunt Esther when I was perhaps five or six. The only things I remember from that day was running toward the corral filled with real live ponies and begging Mom to let me ride.

My aunt was fearful I might hurt myself, but Mom overruled her. I got a wonderful, if short, ride. Later, some fair promoter brought live ponies to Siren, Wisconsin where my Dad pastored a church from 1955 to 1958. Dad bought me a ride.

It was wonderful, though I got to do nothing more than go round and round a ring.

I did not stop with live horses. If nothing else, I rode round and round on the carousel at every circus and fair I went to, pretending I rode a mighty steed.

At my side, I often wore a play six shooter set, for I was addicted to the Western shows, which showed so regularly on TV. Roy Rogers and Dale Evans were my heroes. They sang about God, so Dad and Mom approved of the show. In Clitherall, I even had Roy Rogers and Dale Evans paper dolls.

One day as I galloped about on my make-believe steed and flashed my pistols, Dad watched. He watched me aim and "shoot" down the neighbor boy, a young friend who lived next door to us in Clitherall. Interestingly enough, the church bought the old brick bank building for use as the parsonage right next to the post office where my best friend lived in the back with his family.

"Carolyn," Dad said later that night, taking me onto his knees, "I know this gun is not real, but no gun is really a toy. Real guns hurt people. I don't want you to point a gun, even in pretend, at anyone. Ever."

I frowned. "But how can I play cowboy then?"

"Aim up or down or to one side, but not directly at anyone. I want you to realize that guns are dangerous, and I don't want you to take lightly pointing them at people. Real guns can kill. God wants us to love our enemies, not kill them." His blue eyes were serious. "Do you understand?"

I nodded soberly. I did understand. Never, after our little talk, could I handle my pistol without realizing what a gun could do, and never after that could I aim it, even in play, at another person.

Though I watched all the cowboy shows, I did more than take in the plot. Intently, I studied the way the heroes handled their horses. I watched how they held the reins and how they moved their bodies to get the horse to trot and to gallop. I watched, and learned.

As I grew older, I followed horse racing. I read books on horses and studied statistics. I fell in love with Man 0'War, that great horse who had never run the Kentucky Derby, though many of his descendants had.

I felt a strange bond with horses and each spring I prayed another horse would come along as great as Man 0'War, one who would run all three races of the Triple Crown: the Kentucky Derby, the Preakness and the Belmont Stakes. Run...and win.

There had not been a winner of the Triple Crown since Citation in 1948, but every spring I diligently read about the current crop of three-year-olds. Each year, I listened to the races on my little radio that Dad bought me for eighth grade graduation, hoping for a winner. Each year the failure of a horse to emerge with the coveted crown echoed my own failure to overcome the odds of my walking again. Walking...and riding.

Once walking had come so easily. Once I ran and jumped with abandon, twirling around and around so fast I got dizzy. Would I ever again run, ever again, even walk?

CHAPTER TWO—Cowgirl

Born strong and healthy January 24, 1950 in Warroad, MN, the second child of three, of a minister's family, I often drove my mother to distraction with my tomboyish ways. Even my younger brother could not keep up with my antics as I shimmied up trees, hung daringly from high branches or raced down the street. My older sister Karin, not in the least the tomboy, quite despaired of me.

From as far back as I can recall, I longed for a horse. Desperately, passionately, I desired a horse of my own. I dreamed of being a cowgirl, riding the range or a jockey hunched on the back of a fleet animal.

When Dad took a church in Lance Creek, Wyoming in 1958, I thought I was moving to the closest place on earth to paradise. Karin was less than thrilled to leave our big white house by the church in Siren, Wisconsin for, as she thought, the "wilderness."

The Siren church was not happy to see us go, but the members gave us a send off even they had not intended. The night before we drove away for the last time, the church hosted a going away party for us. Since the church was just a few steps away from the parsonage, Mom left four-year-old

Paul sleeping in his room while we walked over to the church.

There was food and speeches, laughter and tears. Somewhere along the line, bread ran short. Not much remained unpacked at the house, but the groceries in the kitchen and staples in the refrigerator. When mom learned of the shortage, she volunteered to go over to the house and get a loaf of bread.

"No, Ada," said one of the church women, "Let me. No need for you to leave."

"All right. Oh, by the way, will you check on Paul, too?"

"Sure."

A short while later, the woman returned to the church. Holding tightly to her hand was a grubby little boy. To everyone's surprise, the woman was laughing so hard tears rolled down her checks. It took a moment or two for her to calm down long enough for her to explain.

It seems that Paul woke up and, when no one answered his cries, he climbed out of his crib and headed downstairs. It didn't seem to bother him overmuch that no one was home, though that never happened before. It was almost as though he'd waited for this opportunity. There he was, all alone with no one to tell him no, in a dim kitchen of cupboards and counters and a refrigerator all stocked with food.

When the woman from the church opened the door to the kitchen, which opened to the outside entry, quite a sight met her gaze. Using the contents of the frig, Paul decorated the walls, the counters and the floors. He'd smeared and thrown eggs, milk and whatever else he could find…and was having the time of his life. (We won't talk about what he'd smeared on his bedroom walls in the past.)

The good people of the church took it all in stride and prevailed on Mom and Dad not to deal harshly with Paul. Instead, he got to attend the rest of the party, safely under the watchful gaze of his parents and everyone else in the church.

We left the next day, but instead of going right on to our new church in Wyoming, Mom and Dad decided to use the money we'd received as a parting love-gift to take a vacation. First, we drove down to Texas and on through Arizona and New Mexico where we visited the Painted Desert, the Grand Canyon and the Petrified Forest.

Driving on to California, we met Dad's brothers and sisters and their families, all but one of whom had moved to the coast years earlier. (Until then we kids only knew his brother Bob and family who lived near Minneapolis.) We splashed in the ocean, getting soaking wet and visited Disneyland. For me, one of the highlights was Knott's Berry Farm where we got to ride a real stage coach and where I got to ride a mule.

This was not an ordinary ride on the short trail provided. No, this mule decided he wanted to explore new territory, so off he went on his own with me on his back unable to make him change his direction. In back of me, I heard a shout and

one of the handlers rushed after us. Taking the
bridle, he steered the reluctant creature back to the
hitching post. I rather enjoyed the whole episode
because I got an extra long ride. Almost as good as
riding a horse—and I was very horse crazy.

Wyoming was everything I thought it would
be. I was deliriously happy under the hot sun with
prairie and low rolling hills stretching away as far
as I could see. I loved the pale green cactus and the
darker green, pungent sage. Loved even the wind
that blew the tumbleweeds head over heels across
the landscape.

Paul only seemed to notice the huge road
equipment along the highway. He'd point and say,
"That's mine. That's mine. I'm going to build
when I get big." (He became a contractor.)

Karin was not enchanted. She didn't like the
barren land, not having neighbors and didn't like
the little white house with its three small
bedrooms, the walk-through kitchen and the
dining-living room combination. She also didn't
like going off to high school thirty miles away in
Lusk.

I didn't like having to share a bedroom with
my neat-nick sister. I liked informal organization.
She demanded perfect, dust-free neatness. I like
the full blaze of sunshine. She preferred cool
shade. Our differences ended up in serious and
regular disagreements. She was the young lady; I
the tomboy—and proud of it.

On the way to Lance Creek, I had acquired a
Zorro hat and whip, which I now preferred to my

six shooters. With the hat, I proudly wore a makeshift cape tied around my neck. Our gate made the perfect steed, but, here in the west, I was not limited to an imaginary horse.

It didn't take long to discover our next door neighbor, Dale, had a paint horse. It wasn't long before Karin and I, along with Dale, who was not much older than me, made a threesome that first summer. We took turns riding his gelding, Rocket. As Karin found friends more her age—she was almost four years older than me—Dale and I became a riding duo. That was fine, for I was jealous of any opportunities to ride and did not like sharing my riding time.

Once in a while we allowed Paul to ride, but he was young and most of the time I considered him a pest. One time, when he followed Dale and I as we hiked in the overgrown field behind Dale's house, I tricked Paul into climbing into an abandoned rabbit hutch and latched him in. That was bad enough, but then I went off and forgot him. Thankfully, Paul was something of an escape artist and managed to find a way out all by himself. I always felt bad about that less-than-stellar episode.

At school, I met the principal's daughter, Roline, who was as much the tomboy as I. We'd patrol the school grounds, arrogantly daring anyone to cross us.

School grades came fairly easily for me; though I recall the time I came home with a D in spelling. That didn't go over very well. It also never happened again. Mom and Dad never expected us to be perfect, but did expect us to do our best. And they had a good grasp on what that was. Not that I needed much prodding. I liked getting good grades.

In sixth grade, Miss Lee, the one teacher who scared us all half to death, gave me the major part in the Christmas play, "Santa in Blunderland." I couldn't believe it. I didn't think Miss Lee even liked me and here she gave me this huge part. It made me feel she trusted me to do a good job, and I certainly did my best. Memorizing was seldom a problem, (in fact, Dad put me in charge of helping Paul learn his part as an Up-side-downer) but I needed more than the words, I needed to act on stage with a whole audience listening. I thought we brought it off in good style.

Though the sight of Miss Lee curdled fear inside, nothing kept me from standing up for what I believed to be right. One year, the pep squad decided to sell raffle rickets to earn money. After considering for a long time, I decided that this was a form of gambling, and I didn't want to be part of it. My stomach in knots, I hesitantly raised my hand in one of our meetings.

Miss Lee pointed. "Yes, Carolyn."

I swallowed the huge lump in my throat. My cheeks grew hot under her intense, intimating gaze. "I've, I've been thinking about this." Actually, I had discussed my feelings with Dad. He laid out the different positions as well as Biblical verses, and I sensed he was rather ambivalent about raffle tickets. Still he allowed me to make up my own mind. Very typical. As soon as he thought we could handle making a decision, he stopped making pronouncements and simply guided us into seeing the different aspects of the problems while leaving the final decision to us.

At those times, I sometimes wished he'd just put down his foot and say, "No!"—he did that often enough other times. Making decisions was scary. This was one of those times I wished I could have told the pep squad, "My father…" After all, they all knew he was the minister and would understand if I didn't do something over his objections.

Fact is, he was the minister in a town that boasted two churches, the protestant and Catholic, though a priest came through only sporadically for services. Other than our church, the Evangelical Covenant Community Church, and the barely open Catholic Church, were the churches in Lusk, some 30 miles away. Our church became the melting pot for all denominations.

Dad preached a simple straightforward message of Jesus Christ who died to forgive sin and rose to make us whole in Him as we trust Him.

It was a message Mom and Dad both fervently believed. Mom led me to the Lord while we still lived in Siren. While I felt no different after praying and asking Jesus to live within, I determined to follow Him. I tried…and failed… often.

You see, my temper got in the way. Like

when I pushed Karin through the wall of the house Dad was fixing up in Wyoming, the same place, three times. Dad was less than thrilled. I constantly fought with my sister, but I really wanted to do right…like that day at school.

Once more I gulped, quivering under Miss Lee's gaze. "I think the raffle is gambling, and I think gambling is wrong." The words whooshed out. "Can I help some other way rather than sell tickets?" Inside I felt a mixture of dread, relief and nausea.

Miss Lee said nothing. I think everyone held a collective breath, anticipating an explosion. It never came. After a seemingly long moment, she nodded. "All right. We'll find something else for you." That was that. Standing up for what I believed was the right thing to do.

In Wyoming, too, I matured in other ways, other than spiritually and in self-confidence. For the first time, boys caught my interest in something other than a challenge. Ricky, a boy in my grade, held my hand—and I liked it. Tommy, an older boy and brother to my best friend Roline, wanted to kiss me, but sheesh! I was in elementary school. That felt wrong. I said "No" and he moved on to someone more willing. The stand began to cement my determination to keep myself for my someday husband. As my folks told me, I was precious in God's eyes, precious enough to save for the one who would value me as God did.

As I grew physically, emotionally and spiritually, one desire never changed. I longed for a horse of my own so deeply it hurt. Dad told me, "God knows your heart, Carolyn. He knows how long you've prayed for a horse of your own. God is a good God. Trust Him."

That was so hard, especially when I lost Dale as a neighbor and the privilege of riding Rocket. In a tragic accident, Dale lost his father. Soon after, he and his mother moved away. I was glad Dad had words of comfort for the family, because mine were so inadequate.

In 1962, Dad got called to a small rural church in Northwest Kansas, the Lund Community South of Oberlin. Little did I know the turns my life were soon to take.

If I had, I doubt I would have ever wanted to leave Wyoming.

CHAPTER THREE-Shattered Dreams

We moved to a small country church in the northwest of the Kansas, south of Oberlin. The area was called Lund because there once had been a post office there. Now Lund was a community of farmers with a church and a country grade school.

In no time at all, the people took us into their hearts and lives. In fact the first night after arriving, I spent the night with Diane and Julie Marcuson who lived down the road from us. The girls fought over who got to share the double bed with me. I felt right at home.

In Lance Creek our school had not been large, but I had never gone to school in a one room schoolhouse before. Several rows of desks lined the large room, the first grades sat on the far left, the eighth graders on the far right. It was one of the few eight-month schools still in existence.

The teacher, Mrs. Carmen, was a member of the church along with her farmer husband. Tall and gaunt, she had no trouble surveying the room. I soon found she was firm, but fair, and I liked her. Often, those of us who were older helped the younger ones with their lessons. This helped us not only insure we knew the basics, but also taught us leadership and cooperation skills.

There were two other girls in my grade,

Janice Marcuson and Judy Wagner. (Julie Marcuson was one year younger than I, her sister Diane, one year older. They were cousins to Janice.) While Julie usually played with the younger set, Diane, Judy, Janice and I chummed around together. After school, however, I was most likely to find my way to Diane's house as that was the closest farm to our place.

The parsonage, our home, was a working farm with a barn and pasture land and fields that the farmers of the church farmed. For Dad, who loved to garden, the setting was ideal. Before long, he had planted trees and bushes and laid out a monstrous garden plot. Later, we had geese and chickens. Paul was given a pig that was so convinced he was a dog he would even point for Paul when Paul went out into the fields with his BB gun to hunt. Along with the usual cats, which we always seemed to collect wherever we went, we brought two dogs with us from Wyoming-- Topper and her son, Cutie. We had plenty of space to keep them.

"Well, Lord," I prayed. "Look. Here is the perfect place to keep a horse. Lord...please!"

That fall I joined 4-H. I had already been in the program for a year in Wyoming where I learned to sew. As much as I detested sewing, I'd been proud of the skirt I made. I expected to go on with my sewing. What else could I do and still be part of the 4-H program?

But almost immediately on joining 4-H, I learned of a special horse program. Some breeders in the area offered their older mares to the 4-Hers to care for. When the mare was bred, the resulting foal belonged to the 4-Her.

Unbelievably, I was selected to receive one of these mares. At the first of the year, on an unusually nice January day, a lovely Chestnut Standardbred mare was delivered to our house. The beautiful horse was a show horse past her prime and extremely tolerant of a young, inexperienced handler. Unfortunately, my joy soon turned to frustration.

Early in that New Year, I came down with a severe case of step throat that kept me in bed for over a week. Always disgustingly healthy, I hadn't been ill even for a day in over three years. Even then it hadn't been anything serious. Fact is, when I was very young I climbed into bed with Karin who had the measles at the time, and, while it panicked mom, I hadn't contracted them.

Finally, though I was once more up and about, something was terribly wrong. My feet ached all the time. Dad, thinking it was my shoes, got me some big ugly saddle shoes. They didn't help. Momentarily though, I forgot my discomfort in the excitement of having my dream come true. I had a horse!

True Glory Be wasn't technically mine, but her offspring would be. Meanwhile, I had Glory Be to ride. I also celebrated my thirteenth birthday. Those were the high points of the year.

Not long after I received the mare, when I woke in the mornings my whole body hurt, my joints were stiff and sore. At first the pain was minor and moving around made the pain and stiffness disappear. As weeks and months passed, the stiffness grew increasingly acute and long-lasting. With it came deep agonizing pain.

Fear drove me to pretend nothing was amiss. Since my bedroom was in the basement, and I had my own bathroom downstairs, no one else saw me until I looked my best. A hot, hot shower in the mornings helped get my joints working--at least for a while. Swallowing my fear, I tried to carry on "normally," The effort exhausted me. What happened to all my boundless energy?

Glory Be, the 16 hand mare (tall by riding horse standards), became another source of frustration. Every afternoon she patiently waited for the school bus to drop me off, her head eagerly hanging over the corral fence. Every afternoon, I threw down my books and went to pet her.

Not having a saddle would usually not have bothered me. In Wyoming, we thought nothing of riding bareback; did it all the time. Dale seldom bothered with a saddle for Rocket and neither did I. Now with every joint aching, the very thought of crawling onto that tall back and later having to jump down set my teeth on edge. More and more as the weather warmed into Spring, I avoided the horse I desired for so long.

The few times I did manage to crawl onto her back, (without help, for I was not about to let anyone know the trouble I was having!) I regretted it. My stiff fingers found it difficult to curl about

the reins properly and, more than once, I dropped
them. More than once, I almost fell off the broad
back. Sliding off onto the ground was a nightmare
that jarred every segment of my body.

Always the tomboy, I despised tears, but
now nights found me weeping as I cried out to God
for answers, for healing. I was relieved when
Glory Be was taken away to be bred. At least I
didn't have to feel guilty about not spending time
with her.

In time, I found my efforts to appear normal
had failed.

My teacher could not help but notice the girl
who usually loved to run and race and play,
practically begging to sit inside and study during
recess. Not hard to see something was wrong when
the very act of lifting my hand to answer a
question brought on a grimace. My parents waited
until the end of the 8-month school year to
approach me.

Dad told me quietly he was taking me in to
see the doctor. Turned out it was Glory Be's owner
and, though he was an older man and a kind,
compassionate doctor, the examination was an
embarrassment to a maturing, modest young
woman. Unable to decide whether my problem
stemmed from Rheumatic Fever or Rheumatoid
Arthritis, the doctors advised hospitalization.

The news came as a shock, but still I
remained optimistic. Looking back, I'm convinced
Dad, who'd been a medic in the army during
World War II, understood a lot better than I what

the future might hold. As we walked downtown after the doctor appointment to find Mom who had been shopping, Dad took my arm and escorted me into a small cafe on Main Street where he treated me to an ice cream cone.

It was a singular treat, for Dad was very health conscious, long before it became fashionable, and ice cream was not generally on his list of healthy foods. He smiled, but there was a sadness about him, too.

A week later, I began to understand when I was diagnosed with a severe case of Juvenile Rheumatoid Arthritis (JRA). For me, the long-term prognoses on such a severe case was poor.

I was a fighter. Swallowing my fright, I prepared to fight the hardest battle I had ever fought. I was prepared to fight, and to win—on my terms.

CHAPTER FOUR-Why Me God?

I returned home discouraged, but determined not to let this get the better of me. And yet, with each passing day I got weaker, stiffer. My appetite fled.

On the advice of one of the chiropractors Dad took me to see, I was put on the first of several diets Dad tried out. This one dictated only chicken and fish for meat, and then they could only be baked or boiled. Along with this, I could not have refined sugars and fruit was limited. Vegetables were not.

The hen house was filled with chickens given to us by the generous people of the church. After a while, the very thought of chicken made me nauseous. However, I felt more alert than I had for a long tine, but that only meant I felt the pain all the more. Pain was acute, and at times, I woke up crying and screaming in the middle of the night.

Despite everything we could do, my straight fingers began to curl up, my legs pulled up until I could no longer straighten them. What frightened me most was the speed in which it all happened; happened despite exercises and efforts to keep mobility in my limbs.

Nine months later, Dad brought home a wheelchair, and I cried like a baby. From the first I hated that chair, the symbol of my dependence. Never, never would I give in to this. I would walk again. I would! But even my declarations sounded hollow in the months and years that followed. Not only did I become very dependent, but eating became a chore. I lost sixty pounds, leaving me looking like a living ghost. My sister Karin cried every time she came home from college in McPherson, KS for a visit.

Paul was confused by my volatile, uncertain moods. One moment I was the carefree playmate he remembered, the next I would be snarling at him, screaming even, for him to leave me alone. I was as confused as Paul. How could I know that it was more than tearing, searing pain that drove me? Inside I was growing up with all the volatile emotions that characterize the teen years. I also came to understand that depression and moodiness comes with chronic illness, something I learned from a book of fiction—not from doctors.

Then began the years of hospitalization, diets, exercise, and often strange, and not so strange, treatments. The one constant was prayer, not only those of my parents, but also those of our church family and others around the country.

My own prayers seemed ineffective as the pain took over my life. In the middle of the night when throbbing pain woke me, I often found myself damp with sweat from nightmares that terrorized my dreams. Fear and thoughts of suicide hovered in my pain-ridden mind. Why should I go on? How could I live like this? What sort of future did I have?

From the porch, I often despairingly watched Glory Be contently grazing, growing round and fat. The foal was due the next June. Would I be ready to care for the horse I had prayed for, for so long?

Vainly I struggled to do for myself, but the smallest attempt, more often than not, ended in defeat. I could not reach my head. I could not bend to touch my toes. My shoulders moved stiffly and my legs no longer straightened. My fingers were now gnarled and grotesque and nothing… nothing seemed to stop the relentless advance of the disease.

My fears did not ease with hospitalization. In one rehabilitation center in the south, I fought against going to the lunchroom where the crackers and bread products had been invaded by little wriggly worms or other less-than-appetizing—and often living--insects. Before eating lettuce or any other produce, my roommates and I searched carefully for any type of crawling beasty. Needless to say our appetites suffered.

The slender porter assigned to our ward was an elderly man regularly fired for drinking on the job and regularly rehired in a day or two. He began drinking before coming to work and continued throughout the day, making little effort to hide his habit.

As we were not encouraged to do for ourselves, this man carried us in and out of bed, in and out of our wheelchairs, stumbling as he did so.

He pushed us down the halls, into elevator doors, and, often crashed us directly into walls. Every time He lifted me, I tensed, expecting the shock of pain that came as he caught one or another part of my body on edges of furniture or on partition corners. I felt totally helpless, alone and afraid.

Worse, the powers-that-be put me on some experimental medicine which they assured my parents would act like aspirin. It didn't. In fact it did not help either the pain or my mobility at all. I felt betrayed.

There were reasons the administration did not encourage family or friends to stay nearby or visit. Several months later when my parents returned for me (something I begged them to do), they were horrified not only at my mental state, but also at my emaciated physical condition.

Battered emotionally as well as physically, I returned home. It was a long while before my nightmares of that place subsided from stark terror to something more tolerable.

"Please don't make me go away again," I begged, not wanting to leave the security of my home.

Once home, I tossed out that expensive useless medicine, hoping never again to smell that smell, but I did. Some fifteen years later I opened a bottle of medicine prescribed for my infant son. The smell brought back all those horrible memories...a medicine found ineffective for arthritis sufferers. Aspirin seemed like a friend.

How often I cried out to God during those

days, weeks, years. My parents, too, sought healing for me through prayer as well as through more conventional methods. Everyone, everywhere, sometimes total strangers on the street, freely offered their favorite remedy, making me feel like a freak at best or that my illness was all my fault. Why, if I just did this or that, I would be fine in no time. Father, in desperation, even tried a few of these unconventional "cures." I hated them, but those times made me realize how desperate a person can get.

On my own, I purchased a saddle on which to practice spreading my legs with the ultimate goal of riding again, of one day riding my own horse. Even my determination could block out only so much pain as I forced my legs over that saddle leather. I kept track of my progress in fractions of inches.

Finally, Dad drove me down to Texas to some revival meetings he heard about. While the hoped for physical healing did not take place, the congenial, accepting people as well as the up-lifting spiritual environment did much to heal my spirit--until I got home again.

The question nagged. Why was I not healed? Didn't God care? Such questions tormented me especially in the middle of the night when I awoke frightened and alone.

Those nights, just to maintain some semblance of sanity, I began putting my hopes, my fears into words. Poems and songs flowed then as at no other time. Since the third grade I longed to be a writer, but so much had come between me and that dream.

Now I used my nights to compose calling, "Mom, Dad, help me."

They knew what I wanted. At bedtime both my legs and my hands were so encased by wrappings and splints I could scarcely move, much less hold paper and pencil. Night after night, a sleepy parent ambled into my room at my call to write down my latest song, poem, etc. Mom and Dad were amazingly uncomplaining over this ritual.

This exercise also stimulated my desire to write during the day after I finished studying. For while my friends and I graduated eighth grade from our little country school and they entered high school in Oberlin, I began taking correspondence courses at home.

A good student, I rather enjoyed being able to have my classes at home under the shade of the trees near the corral. Taking a break, I moved my head back and forth to get out a kink, smiling as Glory Be hung her head over the fence to stare at me. I liked talking to her, liked even more watching the beautiful bay colt, born June 1965, that trotted beside her.

CHAPTER FIVE--Tongka
And Renewed Hope

Sometimes tears filled my eyes as I watched the little colt frisking around his mother. That colt was mine, really and truly mine! God had answered my prayer. Then I would look down at my body that had been so straight and strong and cried. Not for long. Not when Tongka Wakon beckoned,

The gentle, soft-eyed colt soon turned into quite a little rascal. He loved racing away down the pasture, skidding to a stop and turning around so abruptly his legs sometimes slipped out from under him. The worst trick he began to play was to roll under the pasture fence. After he did so, when he discovered his dam was still contentedly cropping grass on the other side, he'd panic. Blindly he'd heave himself at the fence. Dad usually managed to avert disaster, until the day of the storm.

It happened during one of those lightening quick storms that can come up so swiftly on the plains of Kansas. When the storm hit, the little colt found himself on the other side of the fence. In his terror of the thunder and driving rain, he heaved himself again and again into the ancient barbed wire, trying to get back to the security of his mother. The fence broke under the onslaught. Dad found him wrapped so tightly in the rusty broken wire he could not move. Had Tongka struggled much longer the wire would have cut his windpipe.

My stomach turned sickeningly at the sight of my little colt as I saw Dad half carry him into the corral and set him down. Tongka wobbled. A long cut slashed down his back fetlock, a large flap of skin hung from his near side, and a gaping hole ran directly across his neck. "Oh God, please don't take Tongka away from me, too. Please!"

The veterinarian shook his head as he tended the wounds. "Mighty close shave for the little fellow." He paused as he made another stitch. "Should make it though. Lucky thing you found him when you did, Pastor."

I knew luck had nothing to do with it. "Thank you, Lord." At least He wasn't going to take Tongka away from me. Tongka would live. As Tongka healed I felt a bond growing between the young horse and me. If he could survive such odds, why could not I? I loved him all the more because he was not perfect. He would not make a show horse, not with his scars, and I could have cared less. He was mine all the more because of what he had survived.

Now that my love of horses had a focus, I read and studied everything I could about horses. I checked out every fiction and nonfiction book the town library offered that even hinted of horses. I subscribed to horse magazines. I joined horse organizations, sent for a horse training course and any free information available. I read. I studied. I immersed myself in the material until I became, in a manner of speaking, quite knowledgeable.

I even researched Tongka's genealogy until I traced his roots back to the one of the founding horses of the Standardbred breed of horses.

I also fell in love with Walter Farley's Black Stallion series all over again, reading them over and over. Racing perked my interest and made my blood race. I remembered my childish fantasy of perching atop a race horse, thundering down the track. Those dreams returned as I read the paper and learned of the horses running that year in the Triple Crown.

About that time, my Mom and Dad once more decided I needed more help than they could provide at home. Though I argued and fought against this direction of treatment, Mom and Dad were adamant. This time, we took the long drive to Minneapolis, Minnesota. Only this time it was not to visit my grandmother and Aunt Esther, nor was it to visit Dad's brother Bob and his family. That is, not for me. Instead, I was admitted to Sister Kenny Institute, a rehabilitation center.

From the onset I sensed this would not be as bad as the other place. For one thing my parents had grown up in Minneapolis, and still had friends and relatives who would watch out for me. Secondly; Mom decided to stay on in the city, living with my Grandmother Salstrand and Aunt Esther (her stepmother and half sister). Mom even got a job, which made her feel real good about herself. Dad returned to Kansas to bach it with my younger brother Paul for the months we were gone. Karin returned to college in McPherson.

The Sister Kenny rehab center operated on an entirely different principle from the nightmare rehabilitation center I had endured in the south. Not only was the staff friendly and courteous, but they also encouraged the patients to do everything they could for themselves.

In the five months I stayed, I learned how to dress myself with the use of dressing sticks and to get around by wheeling my chair with my feet. At every turn I was pushed, encouraged and challenged to use what abilities and strength I had to foster my independence.

Relatives and friends visited often. Since there was construction going on in the hospital, Uncle Bob was able to slip up to see me in his work clothes any time he wanted to. I also made friends with patients my age. In all, despite some rather uncomfortable treatments, my stay was completely different from the stay at the center in the south.

For a time, I concentrated on gaining confidence and independence, leaving Tongka and the races in the background. That summer my mother and I became friends. Maybe, God indeed cared. Maybe, just maybe, He *was* a good God.

It was a summer and fall of growing. No longer was death preferable to life. If I learned one thing during that time, it was how precious my life was. Somehow I would walk again, somehow.

However slow and awkward I accomplished

the task, I refused to allow anyone to help me do the things that came so easily to others--getting around, dressing and eating. I started using, as much as possible, the bathroom instead of using a portable potty in my room. By fastening a comb onto the end of a stick at an angle, I managed to relearn how to comb my hair. My small accomplishments gave me a sense of pride.

My clothes buttoned up the front. Slip on boots covered my feet. My sister made me a warm poncho so I would not need to struggle with sleeves.

My pride extended to Tongka, growing into a frisky colt. Delighted, I watched him prancing about the corral. One day, he no longer needed Glory Be and the owner sent handlers to take her to another eager youngster.

For me, as for him, changes were in the offing.

CHAPTER SIX--Meeting the Healer

For all my improvements, pain kept me firmly locked in its grip. At times even the slightest touch or bump was like a brutal physical assault. Screams tore from my tight lips. My body stiffened as my mind tried to shut out the agony.

Pain stymied my attempts to force my limbs to obey my commands. In the midst of the sometimes overwhelming pain, I cried with frustration and anger against myself, my family, God. Why? Why?

Looking into the future, I shivered with fear. Would it always be like this, me helpless in the grip of pain that tortuously racked my body? Would I always be dependent on others for my care, for even getting in and out of the house, in and out of a car? That future was not a pleasant one, and I forced it back in my determination to walk again--one way or another.

My obsession with horses, especially Tongka, helped me sublimate my fear, at least in the daylight hours. Sitting beside the corral, I cheered on my colt, envisioning myself hunched over his withers and racing like the wind. My prayers were pleas for God to intervene miraculously so I might fulfill this dream. I wanted Him to wave a magic wand and restore me instantly. I demanded His attention, now.

Then Kauai King came to my attention. My heart leaped hopefully. Would this year be the year for another Triple Crown winner, the first since 1948 when Citation took the crown? I had the strangest feeling that if a horse again won the Crown, I'd walk again. It was a strange leap of illogic, but it lodged firmly in my mind.

Tense with excitement that first Saturday in May, my little blue transistor radio that dad bought me in Hot Springs, Arkansas for—as he said—a late 8th grade graduation gift, tucked firmly in my hand, I listened to the Kentucky Derby. I pictured the roaring of the crowd, the turns and stretches of the track, the flashing colors of the jockeys. Rapidly the announcer called the race.

"They're off." In my mind, I rode around the track with the horses, bouncing with excitement when Kauai King passed the finish line in the lead. "He won! It's Kauai King all the way."

Two weeks later it was the Preakness, which Kauai King also won. The Belmont Stakes, however, was the longest of the races. At a mile and a half it had proved the undoing of many a Triple Crown hopeful. Unfortunately, it proved the undoing of Kauai King as well. With his failure, my own hopes plummeted, though I knew it made no sense at all to tie my hopes to the winner of the Triple Crown. It was incredible, but I could not shake the feeling I had deep inside about the connection.

At best, following the races were a

temporary respite from the pain that enveloped me. Neither the races, nor Tongka could take away my pain or comfort me in the night when nightmares as well as pain tore at both my mind and body.

In asking, "Why!" I found my Heavenly Father was more than a far off being. The Jesus who had become my Savior at a young age, now became comforter, friend, and listener as my faith moved from my head to my heart.

In the terror of my pain and nightmares, He surrounded me with loving peace. From pushing Him away as either unable or unconcerned enough to help me, I embraced Him. Never again would I deny His reality simply because I could not see Him.

In 1967 Dad once more took me south to a revival meeting, where we daily attended meetings. During each prayer time, I watched Dad's hope rise, then plummet as I was not healed. Again I asked why. For all that I may not be good enough, surely Father was. As a caring minister and father, would not God listen to him?

The last night of the meetings, Dad wheeled me forward only to have the handsome dark-haired evangelist wave me to one side as though he was discarding me while he prayed for the others. Angry and with the stirring of jealousy, I watched others being blessed and healed while I sat on the sidelines.

Eventually, the evangelist moved to my side. Looking down, he smiled. "Young lady, I've been praying and fasting all day for your healing."

My mouth dropped open. I had no idea he had even noticed me in the crowd of needy people. After a soft word to my father, the evangelist laid his hand on my head. It felt heavy and I leaned into it, all my hopes, all my faith focusing to this moment.

I heard the evangelist reiterate that he did not heal. "Any healing." he said, "comes from the Healer—Jesus Christ. Look to Him," he told me. "Ask Him for healing."

Inside, I suddenly hesitated. How many times had I come to this moment only to be disappointed? No, I must not allow myself to hope too much. In my fear, I silently cried out, "Lord, help me. Heal me. Please."

The sounds of the auditorium full of people, the evangelist's voice faded. In my mind's eye, I beheld a large key heading straight toward me, but my view was blocked by the narrow hole through which I viewed the key. As the key fitted itself into the lock, I realized I looked through a keyhole.

Suddenly the key turned, the door swung open, but my view was as restricted as before. I was trapped, trapped not behind a single lock, but behind a myriad of them!

One by one the key moved forward, relentlessly unlocking door after door. I sensed that each one brought my release that much closer. Finally the last door swung open and, for the first time in years, I felt truly free.

The prayer ended. Once more, I began to hear the rustling, the whispers of the crowd, the solemn voice of the evangelist. Opening my eyes, I was almost surprised to see I was still in the auditorium filled with people. The minister had a strange look on his face as though he wondered what had gone wrong. After all, I had not leaped from my chair.

"I don't hurt anymore!" I whispered, realizing, with astonishment, the truth of the statement.

"What did you say?" The evangelist leaned forward to hear.

Excited now, I spoke louder. "The pain, it's all gone!" I moved my arms and legs to demonstrate. For though they appeared as crippled as ever, I could move them without a twinge of pain. "It's gone!" I wanted to shout. Tears of joy stung my eyes.

"Tell them," ordered the evangelist, shoving the microphone under my nose.

Embarrassed, I stumbled through a. few words of explanation ending with, "The pain is gone. It's really gone!" The crowd roared and clapped.

Indeed the pain was gone. Just like that. From that moment, I refused my pain medication. This concerned Dad until he realized I wasn't being stoic. I truly did not need it.

No longer did I awake in the middle of the night screaming in agony. With the constant pain went the frightening nightmares. For a time, I felt wrapped in a cocoon of God's protective love.

CHAPTER SEVEN--Goodbye Tongka

At home I did my exercises with a vengeance. No one mentioned hospitals. My strength and stamina improved, and I became more independent in taking care of my daily needs. Once more I could button small buttons, zip zippers.

However, even the disciples came down from the mountaintop experience. So too did I. As much as we loved our little country church in Lund, Kansas, Dad felt called to a church in Southwest Iowa.

What about Tongka? Though the church sat on five acres of pasture land, Tongka needed training. Father did what he could, and tried to follow my directions, but he was not a horse trainer. I was frustrated that I knew how, but could not. By now Tongka, a large three-year-old, could be led around and saddled up. But that was as far as it went. The few times anyone tried to crawl up onto the saddle, Tongka turned into a bucking bronco, rodeo style.

Something else also depressed me. Why had God healed the disease, but not restored my crippled body? Was I not good enough? Maybe I hadn't enough faith? Was there unconfessed sin in my life? I didn't think so.

I wrestled unsuccessfully with these questions that nagged at me more and more, depleting both my spiritual and physical strength. At times heaven seemed very far away, and God's ears closed.

Karin got engaged to a young man she'd worked with at a store in McPherson, KS where she attended college. After graduation, she married Jim Wisdom, once he returned from the marines, and they settled down in McPherson.

The rest of us settled into our small country parsonage near Essex, IA. The school year upon us, my thoughts turned to Essex High School.

After doing my schooling by correspondence since starting high school, it was both exciting and a bit scary to attend classes in a strange town, in a strange school that required me to be hauled up a flight of stairs in the old, brick school building, and with all new people who didn't know I hadn't always been confined to a wheelchair. The first day, dad drove me into town and heaved me up the flight of stairs. I sucked in a deep breath. How would my classmates accept me?

My fears proved unfounded. My classmates welcomed me and soon included me as one of them. When my classmates realized I had no way to get to the prom banquet, they worked together to see I got to the dinner. One loaned me a dress, one came and fixed my hair and the guys argued who would have the privilege of picking me up. My high school years at Essex were more than I could have imagined.

Two years later I graduated 5th in the class and was listed in Who's Who.

Tongka spent part of this time in Wisconsin as a stud for the mare of a penpal friend. There seemed little else to do with this rangy, aggressive, essentially unbroken animal. On Dad's salary, hiring a trainer was out of the question. He was still paying off on hospital bills for me. What was the use anyway? There seemed little possibility I would ever ride again or ever walk.

That's when Karin and Jim stepped in. They knew of a trainer in Kansas, and they were willing to foot the bill for training. With renewed hope in the future, I waved goodbye to my horse.

That fall I enrolled in a nearby junior college. (Dad drove me back and forth.) I loved college. Both students and professors were very considerate of me and helped me get around campus. While I immersed myself in classes, dissension erupted between the church leaders and my father. In time the conflict proved so severe, my father was asked to leave the church.

By the end of my first year of college, we were without both a church and income. In fact, there was no other church of our denomination open at that time in the Midwest District. My parents felt their next consideration was to find an accessible college for me to attend.

Mom packed a lunch, and she, Dad, Paul and I began a drive across Nebraska to Scottsbluff where Dad thought a church might be available.

There was also a four-year-college in the town.

On the way we stopped in Kearney, Nebraska. Needing something from the grocery store, we stopped beside the large, fairly new red brick Safeway store situated close to the main highway. After Mom came out with her purchase, and, not knowing the town, we ate our lunch right there in the parking lot. It was somewhat of an adventure to hand food back and forth across the front seat. As always, Mom's fried chicken was delicious.

Afterward we visited the local college, Kearney State College, that offered a journalism program. The people were kind and helpful, and I was able to speak with someone in the journalism department. I almost hated to leave, but we had an appointment in Scottsbluff.

Mid-afternoon we were once more on our way, but the trip proved futile. Our contact in Scottsbluff was a couple who were both open and friendly. "But," they said sadly, "the church, ripe with dissension, has closed,"

I knew Dad was disappointed, and, though I felt for him, I was glad I would not be attending college in Scottsbluff. I had not much liked either the look of the place nor the studies offered. How much different I felt about Kearney State College.

Fact is, Kearney drew all of us. With no church in the offing, Mom and Dad opted to move to where I could get the best education, and where I could get around with relative ease—relative is the term as I discovered later, very relative. Dad would worry about work once we arrived. Looking back, I can see this as a real step of faith for my parents who had few resources, and, because of me, lots of outstanding bills. But we moved.

Before college started in the fall I was enrolled at Kearney State College, Kearney Nebraska. I felt I had come home.

Dad began selling water softeners. Mom got a job working part time at a used clothing store downtown. Paul and I attended school. We found friends at the local Evangelical Free Church, a church similar in beliefs to our own. Just as we got nicely settled in, Dad got called to a country church in Ontario, Canada north of where he had served once long before; just north of where I had been born. There was little thought of Dad turning down the offer. The jobs he tried in Kearney didn't pay the bills. Besides, God called him to be a minister.

On discovering the church was not only far from a college, but also from a high school, Mom and Dad elected to keep our home in Kearney. Dad moved to Canada alone, coming home whenever he could.

We lived in a big, old house with all upstairs bedrooms. Of course, this would not do for me, and Mom fixed up my room downstairs in what had usually been used as a laundry room. Conveniently, a downstairs bathroom opened off my room. Mom often slept downstairs on the couch, I think, to be near me.

One Saturday night, in the darkest part of

night as it headed into Sunday morning, a knock sounded at the door. Frightened, Mom scurried into my room. "Someone's at the door,"

"Answer it." I sat up.

"Are you kidding? At this time of night?" We had seen and heard more than a few strange things going on in the neighborhood before, and Mom certainly did not want to admit some "nut," as she put it into the house.

"Just peek out the window."

This she did. Suddenly I heard her glad cry, and the front door creak open. A deep voice of welcome made me smile. Dad was home. Turned out he returned home to surprise Mom for Mother's Day. He'd certainly done that!

The next summer Mom and I went up to Canada for an extended visit. Though we missed Dad after our visit up north, I was thankful Mom and Dad decided to put down roots in Kearney. In fact, Mom and Dad bought an almost new house not far from the house we'd rented. It was the first home Mom had ever been able to call her own. She felt settled and secure. This was the home where they would spend their retirement years.

I was enjoying my classes, especially those in journalism, my major, though I was continually frustrated by my inability to get around campus by myself and depended upon other students, teachers and Good Samaritans to assist me. Still. I found the students even faculty, usually willing to lend a hand pushing my chair.

That first summer in Kearney I visited Karin

and Jim in McPherson. They took me to see Tongka, who had gone from a bay to a beautiful iron gray. But, they could no longer afford to keep him, and I no longer had the option to keep him myself. Sadly, I allowed his trainer Mr. Paul to sell Tongka east for a polo pony. However, my time at his facility netted me enough information and photographs to write an article I sold to Grit. That was a heady experience.

For several years after Tongka went east, I dreamed of going in search of him--after, of course, I started walking again. Over and over I concocted tableaus in which Tongka and I were joyfully reunited. Unknowingly, in the process, I honed my skills as a story teller and as a writer, skills also honed in my college classes.

In our church in Iowa I had met Margaret Freeman from our church. She was quite the author with stories, articles, program material and even books to her credit. She took me under her wing. Under her tutelage, I sold a couple of short stories to children's Sunday School papers.

Back in Kearney, after my visit to Canada, I used my acquired skills to write a story about the young people who took time out of their summer to come up from the states to help out at the church while we were there. I sold not only the article, but pictures as well.

My thoughts turned more and more to writing. But neither horses nor my love for them was forgotten.

CHAPTER EIGHT--The Last Christmas

Now the only horses to hold my attention were the horses running in the spring. Each year, with the blooming of the flowers and the budding of the trees, I felt drawn to those three important thoroughbred races which comprised the Triple Crown. Each year not a horse stood out; not one horse proved his mettle to wear the crown. Somehow, I felt their failure signaled my continued tie to my chair. Silly, yet...

At college, I made friends who accepted me for what and who I was. Before long, I had a group of guys and gals I called friend, friends who confided in me, joked with me, and took me places. They muted the hurt when others saw my wheelchair as a barrier to offering the assistance needed to make me part of their group. My female friends and I enjoyed talking and hanging out. Dating wasn't a huge issue since many of my friends were part of the Navigator group that discouraged one-on-one dating during the college years. Still, while my male friends thought of me as a confidante, they did not seem to consider me as a possible date—then or ever.

It did not take me long to conclude I would never know the joys of marriage or children, never know the love that only a loving mate offers.

Confronting reality hurt, and I poured out my feelings in my writing. By this time, I had sold several short children's stories and articles, and had begun selling program material.

There was also, Al. Tall, blond, and aggressively outgoing, he and I hit it off immediately. Both of us had been voted in on our church youth planning committee. We spent much time together with the other two members. He also swept me into his group of friends, among whom were Keith, Jeff, and Lee.

Jeff had the only car in the group, an old clunker we called the "Tank." Whenever we hit a bump, those of us in the back were bounced to the ceiling. Other times, he drove backwards when the car refused to go forward. The Tank was like another friend.

Those years I laughed as I hadn't laughed for a long time. All made sure I was even included in the Navigator spring break outing to the Ozarks. For a time, though Al often frustrated me to the point of fury, I tried to convince myself there was more to our relationship than mere friendship. But I was too practical not to know the truth. However much my natural desires clamored to be appeased, I had seen the result of dating and marrying out of God's will. Al was not God's will for me, and I knew it. (Sheesh! We would have been a horrible match.) We remained what we'd always been—friends.

The next year, he excitedly told me of his engagement to a lovely Christian girl named

Delores. I felt no jealousy. I had already let go my feelings for him, and I wished him God's best. He and his wife (a nurse) ended up becoming missionaries, serving with Wycliff Bible Translators at a school for missionary families (MKs) both in Indonesia and in the Philippines.

As Al spent his time with Delores, Keith, Jeff, and I spent more time together, growing close as friends. I needed friends. I didn't know then how much I would need these friends in the next two years. I did know that graduation was fast approaching, and I had no idea what I would be doing after graduation.

I dreamed of being editor at some publishing house, but here I was still bound to my chair. I could not even get around without help. The future scared me.

In December, Mom convinced me to go in to see Dr. Ken Ellis, an orthopedic surgeon and an acquaintance from church. After a thorough examination, he suggested the possibility of surgery. I shied skittishly from the suggestion, but the thought refused to go away. I hated the idea of being incarcerated once more in a hospital where my wishes would often-as-not be ignored, my modesty mocked, and my limited independence curtailed. I put off the decision until after the holidays.

Christmas was Mom's favorite time of year. She loved the smells, loved making or choosing just the right gifts, loved decorating, loved the carols, which she played with such finesse on her piano. As always, she baked cookies galore, making plates of goodies for half the neighborhood. She also made beautiful whipped candles as gifts. Oh how she loved Christmas. This Christmas would be different and it saddened her. Karin and Jim, who had moved to Maryland in the fall, were spending Christmas with his family in Kansas before coming to Kearney.

Since they were having Christmas there, we planned to postpone celebrating our Christmas until they came to Kearney later in the week. Though it made Mom sad not to have Karin home for Christmas Eve, she tried not to let it get her down.

December 23rd, though she seemed more tired than usual, Mom gaily decorated the tall, fragrant pine tree Paul set up in the corner of the living room. Outside, the wind howled. Snow snaked in whenever someone opened the door. This time when the door swung open, it wasn't Paul already home from work or a neighbor, greeting us with "Merry Christmas."

A hearty, "Anyone home?" brought Mom on the run. Laughing, she flung herself into Dad's arms. Except for Karin, our family was now complete.

After supper, as usual, we had family devotions about the table. We were thankful to be together. With Dad's amen still ringing in the air, Mom slumped over and slid to the floor.

Dad squatted on the floor beside Mom's

limp body, and though he'd once been a medic behind the front lines in WW II, this left him too shocked to be of much help. Paul took charge. Paul commanded me, "Call the emergency unit." That semester at college, he'd taken two life saving courses. As he'd been taught, Paul began artificial respiration. However, Paul's heroic efforts to revive Mom failed, as did those of the emergency unit, which came quickly to the scene.

As the crew carried Mom from the house on a stretcher, followed by Dad and Paul, I backed up to the Christmas tree, shivering uncontrollably. Soon concerned neighbors peeked in the still open front door. JoAnn closed the door and sat with me. Fear knifed through a body that seemed frozen inside.

It seemed forever, but finally Dad and Paul returned home. They came to notify Karin. Knowing Karin could not handle the terrible prognosis, Dad asked to speak to Jim. But Karin, descending the stairs in the house where they stayed, heard Jim's side of the conversation and began to scream. They left McPherson immediately and arrived at the house during the night. By then, the pastor's wife and my friend, Lois McNeil, waited with me. Prayed with me.

When Karin and Jim and their little dog arrived, I got up not having slept. Tears streaked Karin's pale cheeks. After a quiet greeting and shushing their little dog who didn't understand, and after a hug, Karin and Jim drove to the hospital.

Mom never regained consciousness. She'd had a massive stroke, and we were forced to let her go. The next afternoon, Christmas Eve day, she passed away. That evening, we celebrated Christ's birth in a very subdued manner. Quiet smiles mingled with lots of tears. Every gift held special meaning, especially those gifts chosen by Mom. It was as though she sensed she would not be with us much longer. Yet, while she was not with us physically, I sensed her presence. After all, was she not now with the Lord?

For Karin, it was hardest of all, and she chided herself for not spending Christmas at home —a first. Further, she and Jim had kept a secret. When they came for Christmas, they had planned on telling Mom she was getting her dearest wish— a grandchild. Mom would never know her grandchildren, and it broke Karin's heart.

"Where are you, Lord?" I railed at Him. The question, "Why? Why?" rang over and over inside, but He did not seem to hear. Maybe He did not even care. No, that was wrong, but...

CHAPTER NINE-He's In Control

Christmas and the ensuing funerals over, (one in Kearney and one in Lund, Kansas where Mom was buried), Karin and Jim returned to Maryland, and Dad returned to his ministry in the north. Paul and I coped with our grief alone, though not completely alone, for the neighbors and our church did what they could to help and support us through our grief.

Still, I moved about in a fog. Nightmares once more invaded my nights, leaving me listless and exhausted. The Bible was a closed book, but verses I had memorized long before played in my mind to sustain me.

My grades plummeted and the decision regarding surgery became a painful contemplation. It was hard to care--about anything.

The house was fixed up so I could pretty well manage on my own, though often Paul was pressed into service. He was unusually patient during that time. He even put up with my fumbling attempts to cook, though I'm sure he was thankful for his meals at the restaurant where he worked.

Why? Why? Would I ever stop asking? At school, a couple of months later, my journalism counselor took me to task. "Carolyn, if the faith you've been living here at college is real, you'll get through this."

His statement hit home. My feeble efforts at witnessing had been noted. Tears stung my eyes. Once more, I envisioned a large key unlocking a lock and a door swinging open. The warmth and light of God's presence filled me, chasing away the last of the cloying fog. For the first time in mouths, I wanted to laugh. God had been with me all along holding tightly to my hand, gently chiding. "My child, will you not trust me fully yet?"

So I looked to the future and surgery. Dr. Ellis, the surgeon, became a close friend as he patiently answered my questions and helped me to a decision. He personally, along with a few others, found funding for the expensive surgeries required.

My crippling was severe and my young age was a strike against me, because total knee replacements were then not guaranteed to last more than ten years. There was also no guarantee that the surgery would be what I envisioned. Dr. Ellis commented dryly, "Can't make you much worse!"

It did not come together easily. Hesitant himself over the surgery, Dr. Ellis took my x-rays (at his own expense) to the founders of the technique. There were problems getting my surgery paid for, problems with getting the proper parts for my small legs.

Waiting was hard. The races helped divert my attention. The name Secretariat caught my attention. The bright red chestnut, with three white feet and white down his nose, brought forth that sense of bonding I'd once felt toward Kauai King. With renewed hope, I latched onto his potential,

The first Saturday in May I sat with my faithful little transistor radio on the edge of my bed. First time about the track my stomach turned sickeningly. Secretariat was dead last! I tensed as he began to move up. Screaming, I bounced up and down on the bed as Secretariat passed the leaders winning handily by 2 1/2 lengths.

If Secretariat could come back so strongly after his defeat in the Wood Memorial then maybe, just maybe, there was hope for me. Listening to the Preakness, the shortest of the races, I was pretty confident. To my delight, Secretariat won it handily,

Apprehensively, I looked forward to the Belmont Stakes, Would Secretariat fall back as had Kauai King? Would Secretariat prove to be a stayer for the longest race in the Triple Crown? Or would he, too, fail as had so many others, to win that coveted Triple Crown?

Temporarily, I put my interest on hold as I graduated from Kearney State College, KSC. Though I never fully recovered the grade point average I'd held before Mom's death, I did graduate Honorable Mention and was listed in Who's Who, receiving a BS Degree in Journalism.

Sadly, I said goodbye to my academic career and to friends going off to work and/or to marry. Many I would never see again. In the wake of taking care of Mom's affairs, Paul and I now had a house that was a liability. Mom and Dad would never retire in Kearney. Paul wanted out, wanted to get an apartment, and we began thinking of getting rid of the house.

Hospitalization loomed ahead for me. Fear vied with the anticipation of walking again. Having no one with whom I felt free to share my deepest thoughts, I trusted them to stories, to articles and to my journal. Though the future possibilities consumed my thoughts, not for a moment would I miss the Belmont Stakes.

Inside I could scarcely contain my excitement as I closed my door against intruders on this momentous day. My knuckles showed white where they gripped that little blue radio. "Please God!"

Then the shout, "They're off!" Secretariat sprinted into the lead.

"No! NO!" I groaned, thinking he was destroying his chances in a premature bid for the lead. Maybe, after all, the rumor that Secretariat was nothing but a speed horse, a sprinter, were true.

"Take it easy," I muttered. I listened in amazement as Secretariat ran the fastest six furlong race in Belmont history. "He still has half a race to run!" I cried. Tense, I waited for him to stumble, pull back in exhaustion, but it did not happen. Stretching out, Secretariat raced on, increasing his lead with every stride. The announcer was beside himself with excitement. The crowd surged to its feet, roaring their encouragement.

Thirty lengths in front of the other horses, Secretariat passed the finish line, clipping the 2:26 3/5 record to 2:24. Forever he won himself a place in history—and in my heart.

Exhausted, I slumped back against my pillow and let tears, which I had held back for so long, fall. He won, becoming the first Triple Crown Winner since 1948.

"Oh. Lord," I prayed. "Make me a winner, too. Whatever happens, help me not to quit." In time, a peace settled into my heart about the operations to come. I would make it. This determination differed from the stubbornness that characterized my battle for wholeness up to this point. The person that emerged that afternoon was not the same one that always demanded, "Why!"

Somehow, Secretariat's victory showed me more than any sermon that God, not me, was in control. This time, my determination to walk was tempered with the realization that God had plans of his own for my life, as well as His own timing.

"All right, Lord. I admit I'm scared. Help me trust you." I soon discovered how much I would need His help.

So with Paul looking out for renters, and knowing I would probably never again live permanently in that house, I entered the hospital. Five weeks and surgery for two total knee replacements as well as other assorted surgeries to lengthen heel cords and hip muscles, left me weak, ill, once more totally dependent on others and depressed by the battle that still lay ahead.

Never had I envisioned the sheer grit it would take just to force my legs to move with the full-length braces, which made my legs feel like they were encased in cement. Long, angry red scars scored the upper and under side of my knees, as well as on the underside of my legs to my heels. Blood ran from the recently lanced pocket of blood that collected under my knee.

Still, five weeks after entering the hospital in a wheel chair, I left--walking. True, I inched precariously along on the leg braces and crutches with the nurses positioned on either side, arms out cautiously, to catch me should I fall. But walking!

My brother waited in his car to take me to my new apartment where a friend and new roommate awaited me. The future stretched out hopefully before me. I was indeed a winner, but not because of my strength, but because of God's unfailing loving kindness. And He wasn't finished yet.

CHAPTER TEN-And Now

It took me almost a year to relearn how to walk. By the time I discarded both crutches and braces, my friends Jeff and Keith and I had added a forth to our group--Gloria. They stood beside me during those long months of physical therapy, night leg wraps (which Gloria put on before returning to the dorm for the night while Keith and Jeff waited in the living room to escort her) and discouragement.

More than friendship came from those months. Fifteen months after my original surgery, and after another surgery in the fall, I walked down the aisle of our church to take Keith's arm and become Mrs. Keith Scheidies. Jeff and Gloria, by then engaged, stood up with us along with my sister Karin and Mark, Keith's brother. (Keith is the oldest sibling of five. Mark is next oldest. The youngest brother, Tim, was our candle lighter. JoAnn's oldest daughter, Shenandoah, was our flower girl and Ken & Carolyn Ellis' son, Jeff, our ring bearer.)

Today Keith and I live in a modest three bedroom house built specifically for me by my brother Paul who became a contractor. (He married a lovely woman, Lorene, who has become a close friend). God blessed us with two children--

Christopher born in 1980 and Cassandra in 1983.

Christopher married Jennifer Jensen in 1999. They have three children: Devon-2000, Dane-2002 and Victoria (Tori)-2004. Chris is tech, audio engineer, a sound designer and composer who has created many of my book covers. He graduated from the Berklee College of Music with a Production and Technology Master's Certificate.

Cassandra (Cassie) pursued her Master's in Counseling, receiving her degree December 2007. She is licensed in both Nebraska and Iowa as a counselor. She married Kurt Hungerford 2015 March 14—Pi day. (They served pie and ice cream at the reception.)

My dad remarried and had many good years with Dorothy until we lost him to a heart attack in his sleep in 1988.

Today, we're also dealing with Keith's cancer. He has responded well to continued treatment.

My writing credits have lengthened through the years. I've had over two dozen books published, many of which have garnered awards. My book contracts included small publishers as well as traditonal publishers such as Barbour and Harlequin. One of my Hub columns won an Amy award in 2013.

I've worked as a columnist, editor, book reviewer (had a site for over ten years), first reader and have spoken to a variety of groups. For several years, I was guest/substitute class lecturer in the media department at UNK, the University of Nebraska at Kearney (formerly Kearney State College), the very college from which I graduated so many years earlier. I've also taught enrichment classes at Central Community College. I've been interviewed on NTV, KHAS and AFR radio as well as in numerous print and online publications and had a monthly book review segment on NTV when I was a regular book reviewer. I have reached many goals in my chosen field.

Over the years, I have undergone many medical procedures. Both knees have been replaced twice, and one, three times. I have also had three hip replacements, and at least two biopsies (both negative), a bar implanted and tied in with my right hip and knee after a femur break, screws in my ankles, caesareans for the children and a variety of other surgeries that pretty much make me metal from the waist to my feet. I also have metal in my neck from my surgery in 2014 that resulted in a 2 ½ month stay in the hospital, a trach and a feeding tube. (I was able to get rid of both a month after going home.)

I have fallen numerous times (I cannot catch myself), suffering more than one major head concussion (brain bleed and skull fracture) as well as other broken bones.

God has seen us through them all. There are few times now I ask "Why?" for I have learned God has His own plans for our lives. His own timing. As He plainly showed me through

Secretariat and the Triple Crown, He is truly in control.

I recall it was with nostalgic sadness I read of Secretariat's death October 4, 1989. He was a gallant horse with a big heart that impacted someone his owners never even imagined existed. At that point, I determined I would live my life with a heart as gallant and without fear, trusting God not just for the past, but also for whatever the future holds.

PHOTO GALLERY

Minnesota

The Family

Christmas 1954

Paul Fredrickson
born 6/22/54
Fergus Falls, Minnesota

Dad

Clitherall

Carolyn, Paul, Karin

Church

Carolyn & Friend

Wisconsin

Fredrickson Family: Karin, Ada, Bill
Paul, Carolyn (Me)

Carolyn & friends

Our family, Gramma, & friend

Oklahoma City. I get to ride a mule.

Wyoming

Fredrickson family: Dad Bill, oldest sister Karin, Mom Ada, Carolyn, younger brother Paul

The church

As Zorro

Me riding Rocket

Our house

Karin, Paul, Me

My rabbit and me

Kansas

Fredrickson family
Bill & Ada, Paul, Karin, Carolyn

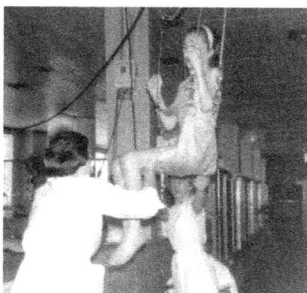

Carolyn getting treatment
Hot Springs, Arkansas

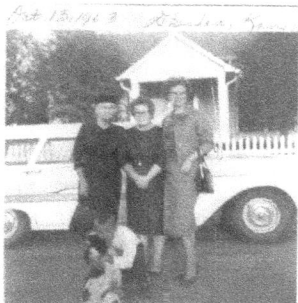

Ada (center),
Gramma Salstrand, Aunt Esther,
Brother Paul & Cutie dog

Carolyn & Glory Be

Dad & Tongka Wakon

Iowa

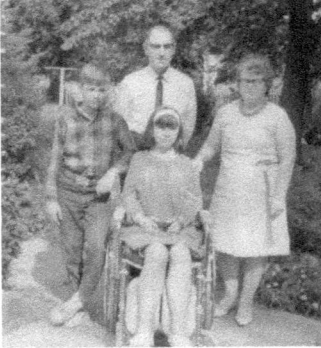
Paul, Dad, Mom & Me

Mom's Relatives Visit

Freemont Church

Freemont Parsonage: Our home

Maid of Honor at Sister Karin's Wedding in McPherson, Kansas

Nebraska

Mom

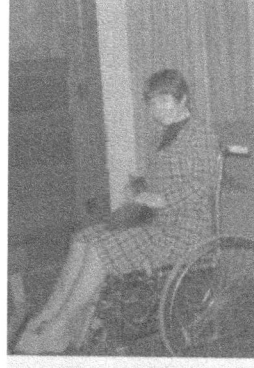

Me

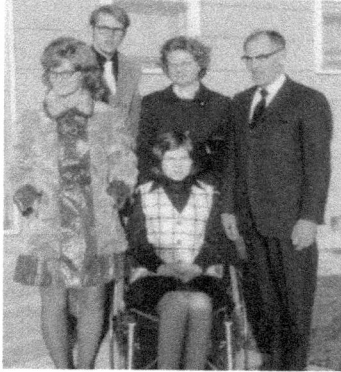

Karin, Paul, Aunt Esther, Dad and me after mom's funeral.
She died 12-24-72

Wedding picture Sept. 2, 1974 with Dad and my step-mother Dorothy,
Me & Keith, Keith's mom Roberta (Bert), dad Lavern (Jiggs)
& Grandmother Fern Scheidies

Daughter Cassie, Step-Mom Dorothy, Dad & Son Chris

Our family at home in Kearney NE

Thanksgiving 1988

Brother Paul & Wife Lorene

Sister Karin, husband Jim Wisdom
Kids: Kelly & Jeremy

Christmas 2004

Keith & me, Daughter Cassie, Son Chris & Wife Jen, their sons
Dane (Dec. 2002) & Devon (March 2000),
& daughter Victoria (Tori) (Jan. 2004)

November 19, 2006

Me with grandkids   Keith with the grandkids
Devon (6), Dane (4), Tori (2)

Grampa Keith & Gramma Carolyn Scheidies with Devon-7, Dane-5, & Victoria (Tori)-3

May 2007

Cassie & Kurt Hungerford's wedding
March 14, 2015, First Covenant, Omaha NE
Keith & Carolyn
Chris & Jen: Devon-almost 15, Dane-13, Tori-11
Sister Karin Wisdom, Karin's daughter Kelly Martin
Brother & wife, Paul & Lorene Fredrickson
(Photo by Jennifer Marcy Scheidies)

Cassie & Kurt
(Photo by Jennifer Marcy Scheidies)

Other Pictures

Bill Fredrickson & Ada (Salstrand)'s Wedding Picture

Keith & Me

Carolyn with Author Friends

Me with Francine Rivers

With Liz Curtis Higgs & Stephanie Whitson

With Karen Kingsbury

With Brandilyn Collins

With my agent & author Tamela Murray / With Dr. Ellis who got me up & walking and who is a character in my book KATALINA, at the signing release of the book.